EXCEPTIONAL LATINOS

FATHER JUNÍPERO SERRA

Founder of the California Missions

Lynda Arnéz

E **Enslow Publishing**
101 W. 23rd Street
Suite 240
New York, NY 10011
USA
enslow.com

Words to Know

beatified—Reached the second step in becoming a saint, or honored person in the Catholic Church.

colony—A settlement in a new area.

convert—One who changes from one faith to another. Also, to change from one faith to another.

dedicate—To commit totally to something.

empire—A large area that is under one ruler.

friar—A man who has devoted himself to God.

missionary—Someone who works to spread a faith.

native—Born in a certain place or country.

novice—Someone who is new at something.

professor—A teacher at a college.

Contents

Father Junípero Serra

CHAPTER 1

Born into Faith

On November 24, **1713**, Miguel José Serra was born on the Spanish island of Majorca (my-OR-kuh). Neither of his parents knew how to read or write. But Miguel José was very smart. Even though he was small and sickly, he went to a good school nearby. It was run by a group of Christian **friars** called the Franciscans. Miguel José's parents also had great faith. They and the friars taught him to **dedicate** his life to God.

Junípero was born in Majorca, an island off the coast of Spain. He studied in the city of Palma.

As a friar, Junípero took a vow of poverty, or promised to live a simple life without many belongings.

At age fifteen, Miguel José went to another Franciscan school in the nearby city of Palma. A year later, he was able to begin becoming a Franciscan friar, which was something he truly wanted to do. He spent several years learning as a **novice**, or young friar, before being allowed to join fully.

When men become friars, they take a new name. Miguel José chose the name "Junípero" (hoo-NEE-pair-oh) after a man who had been a friend of Saint Francis of Assisi. Saint Francis is the Catholic saint who founded the order of Franciscans.

Junípero Says:

"I was almost always ill and so small . . . I was unable to reach the lectern, nor could I help my fellow novices in the necessary chores of the novitiate."

CHAPTER 2

Mission in Mexico

Junípero was serious in his studies and his faith. He became a **professor** when he was only twenty-four and was known as "Dr. Serra" or "Dr. Junípero" to his students. Junípero gave many talks at churches around Majorca as well. Junípero did this until he was thirty-six years old. By then, he knew what he really wanted to do: become a **missionary**.

Junípero left Spain for Mexico in 1749. He and other Franciscans were joining a group of missionaries already working to convert the **native** people of Mexico. Mexico was a Spanish colony at the time.

When Junípero arrived, he was sick. Still, he chose to walk 200 miles to Mexico City! This

Junípero helped to start beautiful missions in the Sierra Gorda region in Mexico. This is the San Miguel Conca mission.

Junípero Says:

"I have been sorrowful because I would have no companion for so long a journey, but I would not on that account turn back from my purpose."

showed his dedication to his life as a Franciscan. The friars had a rule that they must walk wherever they could. On the way, Junípero was bitten on the leg by mosquitoes. The bites got infected and caused him a lot of pain. His leg hurt him for the rest of his life.

For about seventeen years, Junípero worked in the Spanish missions in Mexico. In the missions, the native people were given food, clothing, and shelter. In return, they did work and learned about Christianity. The Native Americans had their own religions, but the missionaries didn't accept them. Junípero also worked at a college in the city of San Fernando.

The Franciscans founded the Alamo mission. They taught the native people about their religion.

CHAPTER 3

The Path to California

By the late 1760s, the king of Spain wanted Franciscan missionaries to head to Spanish territory in California. The king had already sent other missionaries there, but he wasn't happy with their results. In 1767 Junípero was put in charge of a group of friars. Together they were going to start Christian missions in California.

Junípero's missions weren't being built only to **convert** the native people of California. Spain wanted to make its **empire** bigger. The missions would give Spain more power on the west coast

Missionaries like Junípero baptized the Native Americans in California.

Junípero Says:

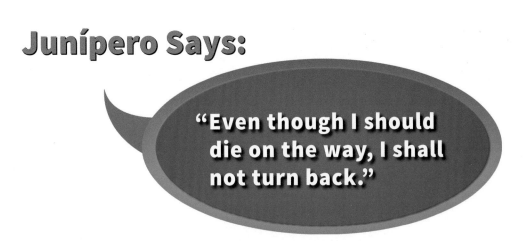

"Even though I should die on the way, I shall not turn back."

of America. Russia was also starting to explore the west coast, and Spain wanted to claim the land before the Russians did.

Junípero's job was an important one. He went with the Spanish governor around the region to learn about the land and the people of California. On the way, the pain in Junípero's leg got much worse. He wouldn't turn back to Mexico, however.

Junípero and his companions met many groups of Native Americans as they traveled.

The Mission of San Diego is still a working church.

In the thorough journal he kept, Junípero said the people were kind and welcoming.

Despite a difficult journey to California, Junípero founded the Mission of San Diego in 1769. He then helped find and explore new parts of the California coast. During this time, he was sick but dedicated to his cause.

CHAPTER 4

Important Influence

Junípero started eight more missions in California between 1770 and 1782. They included San Antonio, San Francisco, and others. The missions made Spain's California claim stronger.

Also, Junípero and other missionaries converted about 5,000 Native Americans by 1784. Junípero believed this was a good thing to do. But many people now say the native way of life should have been left alone and respected.

Throughout Junípero's time in charge of the missions, there were fights between the native

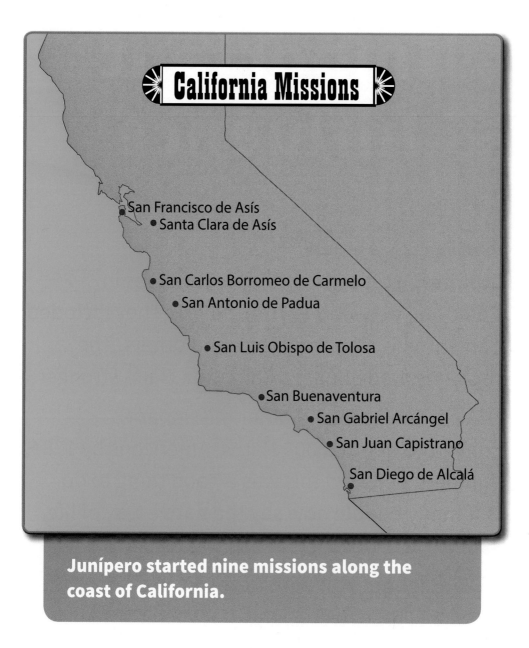

California Missions

San Francisco de Asís
Santa Clara de Asís

San Carlos Borromeo de Carmelo
San Antonio de Padua

San Luis Obispo de Tolosa

San Buenaventura
San Gabriel Arcángel
San Juan Capistrano
San Diego de Alcalá

Junípero started nine missions along the coast of California.

people and the Spanish. Junípero was worried about the Spanish soldiers treating the Native Americans badly. Some people say he tried to bring the soldiers' families to California so they would behave better. He did not think that the soldiers should punish the native people who didn't do what they wanted. Junípero cared about the Native Americans and tried to help them start new lives as Christians.

Junípero's leadership was a big reason for the success of the missions. They supplied cattle and grain for the whole **colony**! However, he was

Junípero Says:

"I pray God may preserve your health and life many years."

Junípero is buried here at the Carmel mission.

removed from leadership when he disagreed with a new governor. In 1784, he died at age 70.

Today, Junípero is remembered for his founding of the missions that would grow to cities in California. His missionary work has also brought him honor as a Franciscan. Junípero was **beatified** in the Catholic Church in 1988.

Junípero spent his life teaching others about his faith.

Timeline

1713—Miguel José Serra is born on November 24.

1730—Miguel José becomes a Franciscan novice. He changes his name to Junípero.

1738—Junípero becomes a full Franciscan friar.

1749—Junípero goes to Mexico as a missionary.

1767—Junípero journeys from Mexico to Spanish territory in California.

1769—Junípero founds the first California Mission, Mission San Diego.

1770-1782—Junípero founds eight other California missions.

1784—Junípero dies on August 28.

1988—Junípero is beatified by Pope John Paul II.

Learn More

Books

Ada, Alma Flor. *Yes! We Are Latinos!* Watertown, Mass.: Charlesbridge, 2013.

Bauer, Marion Dane. *Celebrating California*. Boston: Houghton Mifflin Harcourt, 2013.

Cantillo, Oscar. *Discovering Mission San Francisco de Asís*. New York: Cavendish Square Press, 2014.

Duffield, Katy. *California History for Kids: Missions, Miners, and Moviemakers in the Golden State*. Chicago: Chicago Review Press, 2012.

Web Sites

californias-missions.org

Provides resources to study the twenty-one missions established in California.

kidport.com/reflib/usahistory/missions/JuniperoSerra.htm

Offers further information about Father Junípero Serra's life and legacy.

Index

Published in 2016 by Enslow Publishing, LLC.
101 W. 23rd Street, Suite 240, New York, NY 10011

Copyright © 2016 by Enslow Publishing, LLC

Cataloging-in-Publication Data

Arnéz, Lynda.
Father Junípero Serra: founder of the California missions / by Lynda Arnéz.
p. cm.—(Exceptional Latinos)
Includes bibliographical references and index.
ISBN 978-0-7660-6712-7 (library binding)
ISBN 978-0-7660-6710-3 (pbk.)
ISBN 978-0-7660-6711-0 (6-pack)
1. Serra, Junípero,—1713-1784—Juvenile literature. 2. Explorers—California—Biography—Juvenile literature. 3. Explorers—Spain—Biography—Juvenile literature. I. Title.
F864.S44 A764 2016
979.4'02'092—d23

Printed in the United States of America

To Our Readers: We have done our best to make sure all Web site addresses in this book were active and appropriate when we went to press. However, the author and the publisher have no control over and assume no liability for the material available on those Web sites or on any Web sites they may link to. Any comments or suggestions can be sent by e-mail to customerservice@enslow.com.

Photo Credits: American Spirit/Shutterstock.com, p. 16; Enslow Publishing, p. 18; © iStock.com/FrankRamspott, p. 6; Ken Wolter/Shutterstock.com, p. 20; Mdhennessey/Wikimedia Commons/Canyon of the Little Christians.jpg/PD-US, p. 14; Richard Cummins/Robert Harding World Imagery/Getty Images, p. 21; Toria/Shutterstock.com (blue background); Universal Images Group/Getty Images, pp. 1 (Father Junípero Serra), 4, 7; Wendy Connett/Robert Harding World Imagery/Getty Images, p. 10; William Ludwell Sheppard/Wikimedia Commons/Alamo as Spanish Mission.jpg/Public Domain, p. 12.

Cover Credits: Universal Images Group/Getty Images (Father Junípero Serra); Toria/Shutterstock.com (blue background).